NO WAR ON IRAQ!

THE PASSIONS OF THE PEACE PROTESTERS

IN THEIR SIGNS

NO WAR ON IRAQ!

THE PASSIONS OF THE PEACE PROTESTERS

IN THEIR SIGNS

by Diane Joy

ISBN: 1-58790-073-4

Library of Congress Control Number: 2004092910

All photographs by Diane Joy

book & cover design: Roz Abraham

Regent Press
6020-A Adeline Street
Oakland, CA 94608
regentpress@mindspring.com

On October 25, 2002, Senator Paul Wellstone was killed in a plane crash. The next day one of four large peace marches was held in San Francisco.

I attended that first march to express my grief and to honor the memory of Paul Wellstone, one of only 23 senators to vote against authorizing President Bush's war on Iraq. I joined thousands who marched up Market Street in San Francisco to rally at the Civic Center.

At that first march and the three that followed, the strong personal feelings of many of the marchers were expressed in the signs they had made. Angry, poignant, racy, funny — all passionately objected to the imminent war against Iraq.

It became obvious by the third march that there were recurrent ideas expressed in these handmade signs: that this was a war to control oil; that too many sacrifices would be made, both of U.S. troops and Iraqui citizens; that Bush was a bully and not too bright; and that many in Bush's administration were equally responsible for bringing us to war.

Three of the four San Francisco protest marches recorded in these photographs took place before the war started. For this reason, if for no other, they should be remembered historically.

This, then, is a pictorial commemorative of the peace protesters and their signs.

Diane Joy
Berkeley, California

CONTENTS

To the caring people who showed up for the peace marches in San Francisco, this book is dedicated.

The following were organizers and/or supporters of the peace marches which took place on October 26, 2002, and January 18, February 16, and March 15, 2003. Thanks to them and apologies for any omissions:

Bay Area United Against War
Direct Action Against the War
International Act Now to Stop War and End Racism Coalition
International Answer
Justice in Palestine Coalition
Not in Our Name
United for Peace and Justice
Vanguard Public Foundation

No to WAR...

2

3

15

STOP WORLD WAR DUBBYA

ALL WE ARE SAYING... IS RETHINK YOUR STANCE!

PETALU
Junior Hi

23

YES to PEACE...

35

ANOTHER
GRANDMA
TAKES TO THE
STREETS

FOR THEM

AND FOR
US ALL
PEACE

38

40

41

WORDS to LIVE BY...

An eye for an eye would blind the World – Ghandi

HE'S NOT MY PRESIDENT

see appendix

47

48

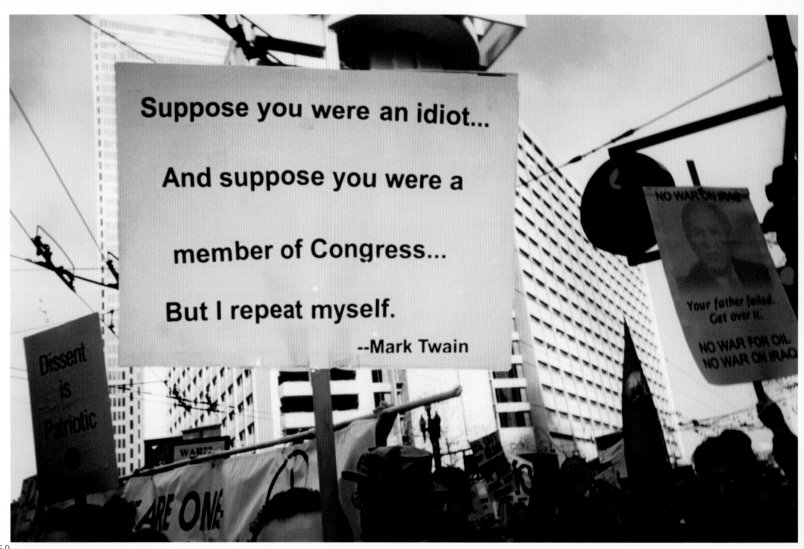

VIEWS of AMERICA...

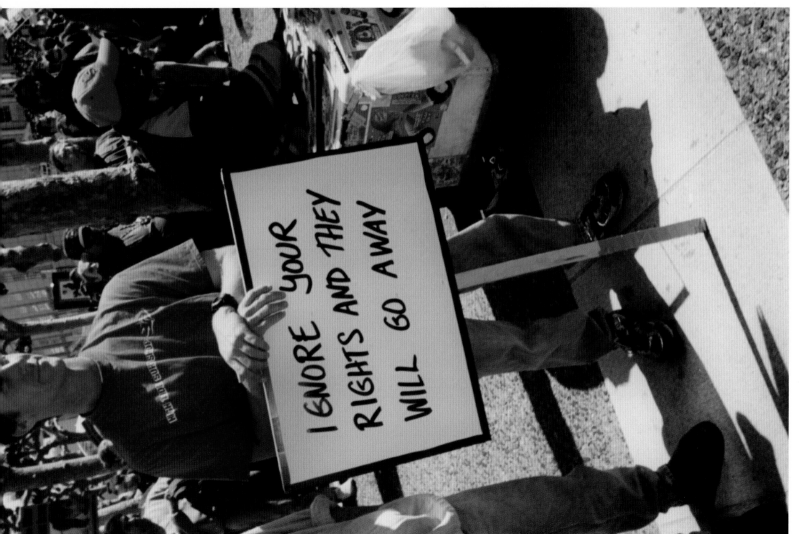

LET'S CHANGE THE
BILL OF RIGHTS
TO THE BILL
OF WHAT'S LEFT

PEACE
RIES

IGNORE Y
RIGHTS A

THE MILITARY ISSUE...

THE OIL ISSUE...

NO WAR ON IRAQ

Your father failed.
Get over it.

NO WAR FOR OIL
NO WAR ON IRAQ

ALL the PRESIDENT'S MEN (and WOMAN) ...

see appendix

BUSH AND CO.'S PLAN:

DESTROY THE MIDDLE EAST
REBUILD THE MIDDLE EAST IN THE
RIGHTWING EVANGELICAL MOLD

GIVE CONTRACTS FOR REBUILDING TO
PROFITEERING FRIENDS—HALLIBURTON,
BECHTEL, ET AL

PAY FOR THIS WITH U.S. TAXES
AND SALE OF IRAQI OIL

SCARY SCARY SCARY

see appendix

VIVE la FRANCE, ET AL...

see appendix

85

A FEW REPUBLICANS SHOW UP...

AND ABOUT BUSH...

HE CAN'T
GO BACK
TO TEXAS
THEY EXECUTE
THE MENTALLY
INCOMPETENT

see appendix

112

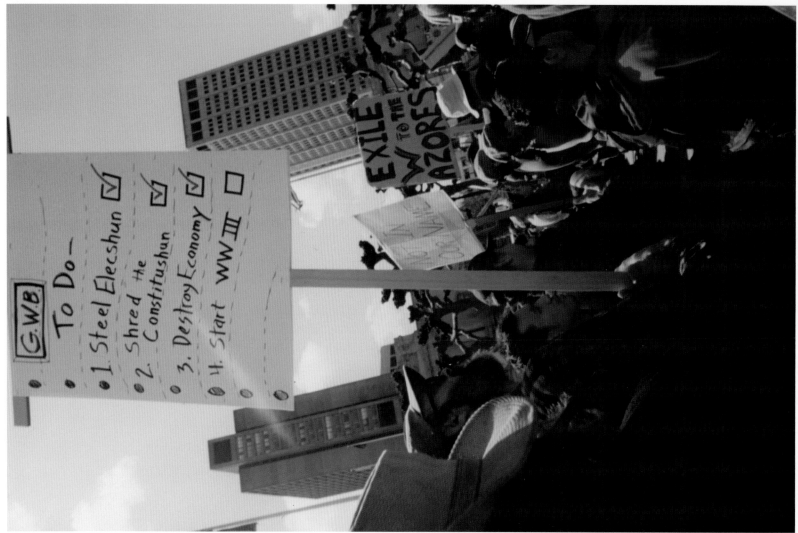

124

SMUGNESS ABOUT WAR
IS **NOT** PRESIDENTIAL

NO MORE OIL

STOP WAR
Against
IRAQ, POOR,
ENVIRONMENT,
ECONOMY,
CALIFORNIA

128

see appendix

131

Appendix

pg. 105   Words under "Homo Imbecilious":
             Though resembling the physical stature of more advanced hominids,
             facial features resembling a smirking modern chimpanzee are
             retained. Homo Imbecilicus is characterized by an extremely
             limited cognitive ability and poor eyesight, mainly incolor
             perception, as it was only able to view the world in black
             and white hues.

pg. 106   Dates under quotes by George H.W. Bush:
                     August 2, 1992
                     February 12, 1992
                     January 15, 1992
             Dates under quotes by George W. Bush:
                     September 25, 2000
                     September 27, 2000
                     October 4, 2000

pg. 131   Find a repressive "govt" that can control and suppress its
             people and Bush and his band of greedy pirates will be there
             to exploit that countrie's [sic] people, land and resources;
             expand U.S. corporate control and arm and support its military
             Terror!
             WE NEED A BIG CHANGE!!